John Dix

A Hand Book for Lake Memphremagog

John Dix

A Hand Book for Lake Memphremagog

ISBN/EAN: 9783337148010

Printed in Europe, USA, Canada, Australia, Japan

Cover: Foto ©ninafisch / pixelio.de

More available books at **www.hansebooks.com**

A HAND BOOK

FOR

LAKE MEMPHREMAGOG,

WITH ROUTE LIST,

BY JOHN ROSS DIX,

AUTHOR OF "PEN AND INK SKETCHES," &c., &c., WITH ILLUS-
TRATIONS, BY THE AUTHOR.

TO BE HAD AT ALL RAILWAY DEPOTS.

PRICE 25 CENTS.

———

BOSTON:

PRINTED BY EVANS & CO., 152 WASHINGTON STREET.

A HAND BOOK

FOR LAKE MEMPHREMAGOG.

CHAPTER I.

Where it is and how to get there. The Connecticut and Passumpsic Rivers Railroad. Scenery on the banks of the Connecticut. Newport.

Something new ! *that* is the universal cry or craving now-a-days. It is so in the matter of travelling, as in almost everything else. Whatever may be the special attractions of any place, in the eyes of summer tourists generally, (poets and landscape painters perhaps excepted,) the gloss of novelty wears off after a few " seasons," and then comes a longing for " the far off unattained and (distantly) dim." Familiarity with " Springs," " Lakes," " Mountains," " Watering-places" and the like, is apt to breed, as in the case of

some of our acquaintance, a species of indifference
approaching to dislike. Even in this great country,
where, travel in what direction we will, there are summer resorts in plenty—each one, as its interested pro-
prietors blandly inform us—" a little Heaven below."
The important question is asked every spring—Where
shall we go this season ? Where *can* we find fresh
fields and pastures new ? Mount Washington, Niagara,
Newport, Cape May, the Mammoth Cave, and many
other " Lions" of travel, have all been " done," and
we sigh like the voluptuary of old, for a " new pleasure." Can such be found ? We answer yes ! Visit
Lake Memphremagog, and our word for it—artist,
hunter after the picturesque, seeker after health, gun-
ner in search of game, angler for trout, pickerel or
longe, bold mountain-climber, strong-armed boatman,
lady wanderer who loves to saunter in verdurous groves
and winding mossy ways—you will, each and all of
you, exclaim after a sojourn on the banks of this lovely
lake—EUREKA !

Supposing the reader to have decided on visiting
Lake Memphremagog, the next thing requisite to know
is how to get there. Fortunately, in these days of
steam, that is an easy matter enough—for one may
breakfast in Boston. New York, Portland, Montreal or
Quebec, and sup within the shadow of the " OWLS
HEAD" Mountain, about twelve miles from the head of
the lake, and in the very heart of its beauties. As at
the end of this Hand Book will be found a complete

table of routes, we will suppose the visitor from the south to have arrived at White River Junction, Vt., little more than 150 miles from Boston, where the Northern and several other Railways connect with the Connecticut and Passumpsic Rivers Railroad, which latter line will convey you to within fifteen miles of the head of the lake, at Newport.

Sufficient time elapses between the arrival of trains from the south, and the departure of that for the north, for the tourist to get a capital dinner at the Junction Hotel; or if he chooses, there is a good Restaurant close to the track. If a stroll be preferred to "creature comforts," the Railroad Bridges and the works of the Railway Companies, will repay inspection. Here White River flows into the Connecticut. The scenery around is picturesque, but the reality of Railways has gone far to banish the "romance" of landscape. If the reader will read the graphic description of a Railroad "Junction" in Dickens' tour of "Two Idle Apprentices," he will get a very accurate notion of the particular one to which we are alluding.

It is one very great advantage of a tour to Lake Memphremagog, that the way to it, for the most part, lies among some of the most charming scenery in the world. The loveliness of the valley of the Connecticut, and the beauty of the river, has afforded many a theme and scene to poet and artist. For a distance of about forty miles on the Connecticut and Passumpsic Rivers Railroad, the track lies close to the river, af-

fording fine opportunities of seeing its placid expan-
sion, picturesque falls, and various windings, as well
as of the verdant intervals on its either side, the mountains by which they are bounded, and the farms and
villages which gleam white among embowering trees
on the gentle slopes and pleasant *plateaux*. But a
truce to anticipation. Amos Barnes Esq., the efficient
Conductor on the line, cries "all aboard," and in
another moment we cross White River Bridge *en route*
in earnest, for the lake;

Now and then we catch glimpses of the river, just
enough to whet our eye-appetite for that which is to
come. One object of interest is a large dam. Crossing Blood brook, the Hanover and Norwich Station is
reached, (4½ miles from White River.) These villages cannot be seen from the Railway, as each lies on
a high table-land about half a mile from either bank.
You may notice on the depot platform, some spruce
young Cadets in uniform, chatting with pale, or merry-
visaged student-looking young men ; the former are
from Norwich University, a Military Educational Es-
tablishment ; the latter from Dartmouth College, (Free
Bridge) at Hanover. Six miles further on is Ompompa-
noosuc Station, before reaching which, we note several
islands in the river. The euphonious appellation of
the place is derived from the fact that formerly it
abounded in wild onions—possibly it was the "Weth-
ersfield" of the Indians. Thetford, famous for its
Academy, is next reached ; then North Thetford, Fair-

lee, Orford, and Piermont Crossing, a quarter of a
mile from which, is the picturesque old bridge over the
Connecticut, (for an engraving of which, see page 11.)

After a ride of five miles we pass Bradford and get
to the Haverhill depot; the village on the New Hamp-
shire side of the river is beautifully situated on a table-
land, high above the stream. Far beyond, is seen
Moose Hillock, 4,636 feet high, the Sugar Loaf Mountain and Black Hill. The river views here are remarkably fine, and the meadows wonderfully verdant, owing
to the frequent overflowing of the Connecticut, which,
receding, leaves, Nile-like, a rich deposit of alluvia
on the land.

Newbury—perhaps the prettiest village on the river,
now appears in sight—Mount Pulaski forming a magnificent back ground to its churches, its well known
Wesleyan Academy, stores and dwelling houses. Here
is one of the best hotels in the State—the Newbury
House, kept by Mr. Nelson B. Stevens. If time per-
mits, the tourist should by all means spend a day, at
least, here, and ascend Pulaski, from whose summit he
will have one of the finest views of the valley and
river. Here too are the far-famed *Sulphur Springs*,
to which in summer hundreds of invalids resort. Near
Newbury is a fine bend of the river called the Great
Ox-Bow, a sketch of which we give on the next page.

Leaving Newbury, we see on our right, in the distance, the Franconia Range, which alone hide the
White Mountains; and shooting along the base of In-

gall's hill, reach Wells River Village, where is the terminus of the White Mountain Railroad. Still running by the river side, we next reach McIndoes, where there is one of the finest falls on the Connecticut. A mile or two further on is Barnet, a place almost exclusively inhabited by Scotchmen, some "cannie" Caledonians having purchased the land on which it stands, years ago, and their descendants still keeping possession of it.

Great Ox-Bow.

Here the track leaves the banks of the Connecticut and goes thundering along the banks of the Passumpsic River, (a tributary of the former,) past McLerans and Passumpsic Depot, to St. Johnsbury, one of the most important places in Vermont. Here is a capital Hotel, the St. Johnsbury House, kept by Mr. Watson. Here is located the world-renowned Scale Factory of the Messrs. Fairbanks; indeed these works and their surroundings, form a distinct village called after its founders, whose vast influence for good is owned and appreciated by all who know them. Fairbanks Village is well worthy a visit; it is the very Eden of Manufacturing Industry.

After passing St. Johnsbury Centre, the Passumpsic becomes so very tortuous that one might fancy a gigantic corkscrew had been liquefied. Just before reaching Lyndon, there are some picturesque falls which will delight an artistic eye. The next station is West Burke, where stages are in waiting to convey passengers to Willoughby Lake, (five miles distant;) there Mr. Bemis keeps a first rate Hotel on the lake's bank. In a short time, after ascending a rather steep grade, the track runs along a high bank at the base of which is Bell Water Pond—a sheet of water about three miles in length, and averaging one in width. It is famous for its longe. At the outlet of the pond is Barton, the present terminus of the Railroad, which, however, will soon be extended to Newport.

There is little in Barton to detain the tourist. Mr.

1

Milton D. Thompson, the very obliging and active Depot Master, will afford strangers every facility in procuring stages to convey them the remaining 15 miles of their journey; or if a stay for the night be preferred, there is the Barton Hotel, where Messrs. Hill & Buck will show guests every attention. There is also a Railway Hotel, but stages run to and from the *former* house.

Immediately on the arrival of the train, stages start for Newport, where we will suppose the reader to have arrived; and now we are fairly on the banks of Lake Memphremagog, which as we descend the hill to the village, stretches away to the north, until in the far distance, it blends with the purple shadows of the surrounding mountains.

Excellent accommodations may be found at the Memphremagog Hotel, which is famous among epicures for its fish. Pickerel, trout and longe are scarcely out of the lake, before, like St. Lawrence of old, they are broiling on a grid-iron—out of the water into the fire, may (to *us*) pleasantly vary the old adage. But we have no time for culinary raptures; therefore let us mount the neighboring hill and get a general view of the lake and landscape—'twill well repay the trifling toil of climbing. This pedestrian feat accomplished, we hear as we descend, the bell of the Steamboat, and hurrying on we soon reach the wharf, at the end of which the " MOUNTAIN MAID " is (for it is 8 o'clock, A. M.) waiting for her living cargo.

Old Bridge at Piermont Crossing.

CHAPTER II.

*Trip on the Lake—Bays and Landings—Passenger
Portraits—Province Line and Island—Whetstone
Island—A Treasure Cave—The Mountain House.*

Here come the passengers by one's, and two's, and
three's, at first, then in groups of a dozen or more—
then one's and two's and three's again—and as the
Captain cries " Let go there,"—the inevitable *last* man,
who (being of a portly and plethoric habit) comes
panting and perspiring and looking daggers at the
Captain, who we may here introduce to the reader as
Captain Fogg, than whom we do not know a pleasanter
or politer personage. In fact he is just the man for
the position he occupies, and so well posted up as to
the lake and everything concerning it, that had he
time to answer all the questions put to him by his
eager passengers, we might as well have left this Guide-
book unwritten.

While the boat is rounding her bows to the north, we
may as well give a brief, general sketch of the lake—
whose name may at first be rather puzzling to tongues
not quite as much accustomed to aboriginal nomeac-
lature as Mr. Schoolcraft. Memphremagog is doubtless a corruption of the Indian name, *Mem plow-bou-*

que, which signifies a large, beautiful expanse of water ;
at least, so says Mr. Pratt, in his *Gazetteer of Vermont.*
Its extreme length is nearly 50 miles—but only a little over 30 miles are navigable by large boats. The
average breadth is about three miles. About one-third
of its length is situated in Vermont—the remaining
two-thirds are in Canada. Three streams empty themselves into it at its southern extremity ; the Clyde,
Barton and Black Rivers. It is also fed by some
smaller tributaries and springs, and has its outlet at
Magog, where it furnishes a magnificent water privilege. It finally empties itself into the St. Francis River, and its waters thus find their way to the St. Lawrence.

We will now endeavor to describe it in detail, by
pointing out as we steam along, whatever may be
deemed worthy of note or comment.

We have not to go far in search of the picturesque ;
it is one great and charming feature of Lake Memphremagog, that its shores, throughout its entire length,
are indented with beautiful bays, between which, in
many places, jut out bold headlands ; in fact, there
is not a " bit" of tame scenery to be met with ; and so
one is spared the disagreeable necessity—inevitable in
some less favored locality—of travelling ten dreary
miles to see perhaps one mile of scenery worth looking
at. Another object worthy of note, and it may as
well be mentioned here—is the great purity of its waters ; you never see weed or scum fringing its shores ;

close to either rocky or grassy margin, it is as pure as at its centre.

At the first glance from the deck of the Mountain Maid, the lake appears as if it were completely land-locked by the mountains within the range of vision; in fact, it seems almost circular, owing to a slight curv-ature, which from this point cuts off the prospect northward. The eastern shore is less mountainous than the western, generally; here it gently slopes to the water, the upland being dotted with farms and pretty dwellings. Right ahead is seen a projecting point, or spur of land, called *Indian Point*, where In-dians encamped as lately as sixty years ago—so at least we were informed by an old gentleman, a native of this region, who well remembered having seen their wig-wams, with squaws sitting in front, making or mending nets. Immediately after leaving Newport, a wooded point is passed, and *Adams' Bay* comes suddenly into view; this is a semi-circular indentation of the lake, and highly picturesque. On the right, and a little to the north, the waters widen and form a sort of harbor, in which is a cluster of small islands, of which those called Black Island, and Tea-table Island, are the most noticeable. These islets, however, cannot be seen to advantage from the Steamboat, but a good view of them may be obtained from the high land near the road from Newport to Derby Centre, on the eastern, or from the stage road, on the western shore.

Other islands are seen ahead, which we shall describe

as we reach them. Having passed *Adams'*, we now
come abreast of *Potton Bay*, (also on the western
side) named after the township in which it is situated.
Here the prospect is extremely grand. On our left,
rises *Bear Mountain*, part of a continuous range which
appears to terminate in distance, in the *Owl's Head*,
which towers above all its aspiring neighbors. Viewed
from this direction, this now famous mountain has a
peculiarly rounded summit, which seems riven into im-
mense fissures ; this bald and craggy top is very strik-
ing, rising abruptly, as it does, from among the trees
that clothe the mountain from the water's edge, to within a few rods of its crest.

But we must not, in our admiration of the landscape,
omit to notice the " figures" which, artistically speak-
ing, give life to our picture. We need not look far for
these ; not further indeeed than the deck of the Mountain Maid, on which specimens of almost every description of the *genus* tourist may be seen. Those two
gentlemen dressed in suits of the true sportsman's pat-
tern and cut, seated on trunks which have evidently
endured much wear and tear, and yet are as serovicea-
ble and strong as ever—who are surrounded with fish-
ing-rods, camping materials, guns and what not, are
evidently a brace of English travellers, who are intent
on " bar," deer, and fish, for the capture of which latter, one of them rather ostentatiously exhibits a book
of magnificent " flies" spoon-hooks and lines, bought
in London, and warranted to " kill." Near them is a

rough looking fellow, whose rifle and shabby fishing-
rod are strapped together; he looks contemptuously at
the blue and red hackle, and the London flies generally, and feels quite sure they wont " du." Nor will
they—for that shrewd Canadian can, with a few feath-
ers, some bits of silk and a hook, make, by the water-
side, a " fly" which shall fall like a snow flake on the
water, and be eagerly snapped at by some deluded
member of the Fish family. That youth with a beard
like those seen in Vandyke's pictures—and clad in
blouse and belt, is doubtless an artist, on the lookout
for " bits," " studies," " sky effects" and " distances."
For a month or two he will wander along these shores,
or on yonder mountains, and next winter we shall see
in the *Post*, or *Herald*, such a notice as this. " We
have just examined with much pleasure, a folio of
magnificent views on Lake Memphremagog, drawn
from nature, by our talented fellow citizen, Salvator
Guido Claude Carmine Esq. They are far superior
to the productions of Turner, Gainsborough, Horace
Vernet, or any of the artists of the old world, and we
hail them as a proof that American painters are superior, even to the much vaunted old masters," &c., &c.
The conceited looking young fellow who now and then
pulls out a note-book and inserts a memorandum there-
in, is a newspaper letter writer, who is prone to exag-
gerate, and deals largely in superlatives. And the
lady passengers! There is among them a whole " bevy"
of beauties—about seventeen young ladies, who with

their Preceptress have come to see the lake ; a more
charming party never danced on the deck of the Mountain Maid. But we have only time to describe one
other personage, and this time, do so " with a purpose."

Do you observe that individual with rather florid
whiskers, who is strolling among the baggage and
freight on the lower deck, assuming a look of uncon-
cern, and yet quietly taking notice of everything ? He
is not one of the crew, for he does not handle a rope
or lend a hand to anybody ; he is not a passenger, for
he looks, without betraying any interest at the
scenery, and is not in tourist costume. He seems of a
misanthropical turn of mind, for he speaks to no one ;
but his want of words is amply made up for by the use
of his eyes. They seem to penetrate boxes, barrels,
bales and baskets. Is he meditating a larceny ? Does
he intend to clandestinely abstract their contents ? By
no means—he is literally and strictly in the path of
" duty." He is a Custom House Officer.

His presence tells a story. The Mountain Maid is
now drawing near the boundary, or Province line of
Webster and Ashburton renown, which separates the
United States from Canada—after passing which, be
you Monarchist or Republican, you will assuredly have
to pay " duty" to Queen Victoria's Government, if you
have anything on which it can be levied—and you fail
to hide it from that lynx-eyed official, who, however,
is polite in the performance of his duty, and gives no
unnecessary trouble.

2

Now just look to the land on your left, and you will
observe a small farm-house ; that is the last dwelling
in Vermont in this direction. A few rods from it is
the small iron post which marks the identical spot
which the Province line traverses ; glance to the right
and you see that you are abreast of an island—through
which also the line runs, and beyond this, far away,
on the crest of the eastern hills, you may observe a gap
through the woods, which indicates the course of the
line in that direction. The iron post is quickly past,
and we have exchanged the domains of Uncle Sam,
for the dominions of Queen Victoria ; we are in
Canada !

Province Island is long, low, and covered for the
most part with trees. It contains about 40 acres of
excellent arable land, which are cultivated successfully,
by Mr. Bavineau, a Frenchman, who, with his family,
being the sole residents of the Island, is " Monarch of
all he surveys." It does not often happen, that a man
by walking a dozen steps, and in the space of half a
minute, can pass from the rule of a President to that
of a Queen. Indeed, Farmer Bavineau can stand
with one foot in the United States, and the other in the
British dominions ; or at will, and at once, place himself under the protection of the wing of the American
Eagle, or the paw of the British Lion.

Just beyond the " line" is *Baker's Landing*—from
thence, still " hugging" the western shore, the Mountain Maid glides onward, while a constant succession

of beauties on lake and land, charm and interest the beholder. The next landing is " Rollins'," which is situated at the foot of a remarkably steep declivity. Here the boat takes in wood, and not a little amusement is afforded by the swarm of ragged little rascals who assist in this operation.

The Mountain Maid, like all other Maidens, now becomes somewhat capricious; and turning her stern toward the eastern shore, crosses the lake diagonally, affording splendid opportunities of views, " ever charming, ever new." The Owl's Head Mountain now looms up grandly, clad in its garniture of living green—its craggy head, seemingly craggier than ever. The deep gorge on the summit is now seen to great advantage, and passengers begin to speculate how far it may be across. Various opinions are given—the truth is, it is about 40 rods from ridge to ridge. Farther north is Mount Elephantis, (or Sugar Loaf) and Ridge Mountain ; and rising abruptly from the eastern bank, Basin Mountain. But on glides the steamer, and *Harvey's Landing*, situated at the entrance of East Bay, is reached. This bay which runs inland in a north-easterly direction for nearly seven miles, is a little lake in itself, and a favorite fishing ground. By means of a creek near its northern end, it communicates with another sheet of water called Fitch Bay.

Near the entrance of East Bay is an island called *Whetstone*, or *Fitch's Island*—(the latter named after a man who once claimed to own it.) This island is re-

markable for a quarry of *Novaculite*, which may be
seen like a yellow line, near the water's edge, on its
western side. Of this Novaculite, capital whetstones
can be made; indeed, some years ago, the quarry was
worked by a Company from Burke, who disposed of
many tons of it annually. So excellent was it, that it
almost drove the famous Turkey stone out of the mar-
ket, and the Company were being amply remunerated,
when from some cause or other, the British Government put a stop to the quarrying; not however in or-
der to monopolize the trade itself, for since the Burke
Company were driven off, the Novaculite has remained
undisturbed. This was, to say the least of it, a "Dog
in the Manger" proceeding. A similar veto was put
on mining on Owl's Head, of which more anon.

Occasionally, when passengers wish to land, or em-
bark there, the steamer crosses the mouth of *East
Bay* to *Magoon's Point*, a spur of land which derives
its name from a farmer who resides on it. This place
has of late, attracted some attention, from the fact of
there being an unexplored cavern in its vicinity, in which
cave, it is asserted, a considerable amount of treasure
is concealed. It is said that many years ago a Roman
Catholic Chapel in Canada, (we believe at a place
called St.. Francis,) was plundered of its treasures,
and that the robbers concealed their booty here. We
are credibly informed that persons are now living, who
saw two massive gold candlesticks which were found
in or near the cave, buried in sand. Several unsuc-

cessful attempts have been made to explore this mysterious place—but it is gravely declared that every
daring individual who descended and penetrated but a
little way, came back in a state of the utmost alarm,
having " heard fearful noises and felt like being chok-
ed," a phenomena which would be easy of explanation
by any schoolboy who had but slightly studied acous-
tics and chemistry—since echoes and carbonic acid gas
would produce precisely similar effects. We hear that
explorations on a large scale are to be made this summer, (1859,) and only hope that the laborers in this
Magog " diggin" will be more fortunate than the san-
guine gentlemen who sought to lay their " appropria-
tion claws" on the treasures of the late gallant Captain Kidd.

On leaving Harvey's Landing, the Mountain Maid
returns to her " old love," the western shore, and zig-
zagging it in a slant direction, northwards, directs her
course towards, as it would seem, the base of Owl's
Head. The mountain now looks grander than ever ;
dwarfing, as it does, all its surrounding brethren. We
can now see the grey walls or ledges of rock which
stripe it transversely ; seemingly impossible to scale,
and ravines and gorges of vast magnitude. About a
mile and a half off, on our left, is Round Island,
to be spoken of presently. As yet, there are no signs
of any " House of Entertainment"—but before long
a wharf with two flag staffs, a pretty summer house,
like a Kiosk—the roof of a dwelling—and then its

front, appears. In a few moments more, we have left
Harvey's Landing four miles behind us, and stand on
the very convenient wharf of the MOUNTAIN HOUSE,
where we are welcomed by the Proprietor, Mr. A. C.
Jennings, who, as former Landlord of the St. Johnsbury House, Island Pond Hotel, and other first rate
Establishments, we had long and favorably known.
Here let us remain for a few days, for this is the Para-
disaic portion of the lake—if where *all* is " beautiful
exceedingly," such a term can be fitly applied. On
glides the Mountain Maid, which we have ungallant-
ly abandoned; but she has plenty to flirt with her
in our absence, and is of so forgiving a nature, that
the paltry sum of a dollar, or less, will induce her by
and by, to receive us on our former (deck) footing.

CHAPTER III.

The Mountain House—Island Scenery—The Palisades Bathing Place — Balance Rock—Skinner's Cave and its Legend.

The Owl's Head Mountain House is delightfully situated on the wertern shore of the lake. It stands in a natural Amphitheatre, on a picturesque little plateau at the base of Owl's Head, very near the margin of the waters. A neat and very convenient plank pathway extends from the front of the house to the lake, and on a wharf at its further end, passengers land as easily as possible. On a rocky knoll is a picturesque summer house ; and back of this a miniature mountain, from whose top exquisite views are commanded. On the south side of the house are flower gardens—rural walks, and rocky pathways ; and on the north, a lovely little inlet with a shingly beach called *Sherman's Bay*, in compliment to the lady Preceptress, who with her charming pupils, visited the house last summer. Between this bay and the house is a bridle path which leads to the summit of Owl's Head. Towering grandly above all, is the Mountain itself, a brief account of which we will give presently.

Taking our post of observation in the little summer
pavilion before referred to, a glorious prospect bursts
upon the eye. Immediately in front rises the *Basin
Mountain* to a height of some 12 or 1500 feet, and en-
tirely covered with foliage. Stretching grandly away,
north and south, the lake is bounded by lofty mountains, verdant slopes, and bold headlands. From this
point, also five islands are visible. Directly in front,
and distant about two miles, is Skinner's Island ; a
very little to the north of it is Long Island ; between
Skinner's and the main land, is Minnow Island ; a
mile and a half distant on our right is Round Island,
and southwards, Province Island, already described.
All these are within a morning boat-ride of the house,
and each possesses attractions peculiar to itself. Suppose we make our first boat trip to LONG ISLAND.

As its name implies, its length is considerably great-
er than its breadth—the former being about one and a
half miles, the latter not half a mile. This Island
is covered thickly with trees, and is chiefly remarkable
for its bold, rocky shores. Near its northern end, on
its western side, are some perpendicular rocks named
the Palisades, from their resemblance, on a small scale,
to those of the same name on the River Hudson.
These are well worthy a visit. Not far from these is a
beautiful, safe, and sheltered natural bathing place.
The shores on the eastern side are very romantic, and
to a geologist, highly interesting. As for an artist, he

might go into fits (of enthusiasm) on beholding the
"rock studies" which abound here.

But the "lion" of Long Island, is the BALANCE ROCK.

Balance Rock.

On the ridge of a granite rock, which slopes towards
the water, stands another huge mass of granite, weigh-
ing many tons, and resting only a single point or pivot,
in the same manner as does the celebrated Logan
rocking stone in Cornwall, England. This one, however, does not move. How it got into its present position is purely a matter of conjecture. Some suppose
it to have been brought on ice, which, thawing, depos-
ited it there. Others imagine the waters of the lake
were once higher than now, and that when receding,
winds and storms washed away the earth which might
have surrounded its base. We profess to hold no

opinion on the subject, and leave the geologist to look
to it. A curious tree grows close to, and leans over
the stone, giving it much the appearance, at a distance,
or in the gray of the evening, of a sarcophagus, and a
familiar emblem. To be sure, one has to *imagine* the
drooping branches of the willow ; but as we all know,
fancy is a very fertile artist, and can accomplish won-
ders.

Leaving the Balance Rock behind us, we now row
to the northern end of SKINNER'S ISLAND, which is not
of so great extent as Long Island, but equally picturesque. It, too, has its " lion" in the shape of a
Cave on its western side, close to its northern extremity. This is a very favorite resort for visitors, and is
easily reached, it being little more than a mile from
the Mountain House, from which it can be plainly
seen. Nearly all such places as these have their le-
gends, and Skinner's Cave is no exception to the almost general rule. But before we relate it, let us say
that the Cave is close to the water on the island side,
is about 10 feet wide at the entrance, from 12 to 14
feet high, and extends into the rock a distance of some
30 feet, narrowing from the outside until the two walls
of the cave meet at the end.

Here then is the legend of SKINNER'S CAVE, which
a friend of ours has " done" into rhyme. It is necessary to preface it with a little plain prose, to render
the verse intelligible. In the year 1812, during the
last American war with England, smuggling was car-

ried on to a great extent on Lake Memphremagog. A
determined attempt was made by both the belligerent
parties to put the illegal traffic down, and one after
another, all the smugglers were captured but a certain
daring dealer in contraband articles, named Uriah
Skinner. This worthy baffled the ingenuity of the
Custom Officers for a long time, but was at last—stay
—you shall hear, dear reader, all about it presently.
After a rather florid description of the lake, our rhym-
ing friend proceeds as follows, in his ruse, which he
calls

The Bold Smuggler of Magog.

*　　　*　　　*　　　*　　　*

In a certain part of this exquisite sheet
Of water, the "States" and " East Canada" meet,
Here, though you can't see it, the "boundary line"
Of Webster and Ashburton passes; in fine,
One-third of the lake's in Vermont, at the least,
The other two-thirds are in Canada East;
The reader must fail not to understand this,
Or the point of the story he'll certainly miss.

*　　　*　　　*　　　*　　　*

Let the reader imagine an Eden-like scene;
Mountains robed to their summits in drapery of green,.

With three miles of calm and blue water between,
And then he will possibly know what I mean :
And the name of this lake, on whose shores neither bog
Nor flat shores are seen, is this,

MEMPHREMAGOG!

A queer word to pronounce just at first, but it slips
In a very short time smoothly over the lips ;
The rhyme forced me to mention the " bog," when I say
You'll be right if you will but the emphasis lay
On one vowel alone—I refer to the A,
And you'll certainly then, not be out of the way.

On this beautiful lake many islands are found—
There is " Skinners" and " Long"—" Province"—"Minnow"
     and " Round"—
On the *first*, will the scene of this legend be found.

When war's dogs are slipped—there is plenty of juggling,
And, among other kinds of rascality—*smuggling* ;
On Lake Memphremagog, such practice was " fine,"
For across it, you know, runs the old Province Line ;
And to dare-devil men 'twas not hard in the least,
From Vermont to slip into Canada East :
Of course, as most matters have *two* sides, we here see
A similar feat might be done *vice versa.*

Now, had *I* such a pen
As has one of those men,

Messrs. Reynolds or Cobb—or Ned Buntline, why then
I'd all of these smugglers of Magog describe;
As I've *not*, I'll take one as a type of the tribe!

Fancy a fellow, brawny and brown,
With very black hair that hangs shaggily down,
With whiskers remarkably bushy and black,
With fists which might give a most terrible thwack;
With very fierce eyes under dark heavy brows,
That flashed like a cat's when it springs on a mouse,
Or like coals in a cavern that gleam fiery red,
With a great roman nose, so uncommonly red,
That whenever he washed it ('twas seldom) I wis,
The water would certainly bubble and hiss!
With a mouth, firm, compressed, and much prone to a sneer,
With a purple scar stretching from chin unto ear;
With a huge dagger stuck in the belt round his waist,
And five or six pistols beside it placed;
With a heavy cutlass not long nor pliant,
Such as little " Jack" used when he slaughtered the " Giant,"
With great heavy boots—and as heavy a purse,
With a tongue that scarce wagged but it uttered a curse!
Fierce as a tiger—as cruel as Nero—
Fancy all these, and you'll picture my hero;
Whose name, for fame has preserved the same,
Was URIAH SKINNER, who'd always on hand
Plenty of articles contraband.

Of all the Smugglers who plied on the lake,
Uriah Skinner was hardest to take;

The officers hunted him often, and yet
Uriah Skinner they never could get!
For *if* his boat they e'er chanced to have sight of,
He vanished, as 'twere, and was speedily right off,
Like the Flying Dutchman, he seemed to melt
Into mist; so that some who pursued him, felt
Inclined to believe he had something to do
With a certain dark gentleman—you know who!

The pitcher may often go to the well,
Yet at last be broken; so it befell
In the case of Uriah—for that bold chap
Was caught at last like a rat in a trap!

*   *   *   *   *

Night on the lake, so clear and calm,
The night breeze sings in the pines its psalm ;
Stars shine bright in the dark blue sky,
And the crescent moon sails in her glory on high :
Above and below, it is all serene,
Who, as he gazed on the peaceful scene
At that moment, would fancy that nine or ten
Very keen-sighted, and well-armed men,
Motionless, and still as the dead,
Were ambushed under the great Owl's Head?
And their ears were open as well as their eyes,
Listening and looking alike for a prize;
There they watched to catch the first glimpse or note
Of Skinner, expected that night in his boat.

" Look—don't you see !
That, Skinner must be !"
Oh, Skinner ! bold smuggler ! there's peril for thee !
For down to the shore with leap and bound,
The officers rush—as goes a blood-hound
On a fugitive's track when the scent is found !
The boat is manned, and they're off the next minute,
They see Skinner's boat, and Uriah S. in it ;
Now the chase grows eager and hot,
And Skinner himself thinks so too, I wot,
For his boat speeds over the waters blue,
Swiftly as flieth an Indian's canoe,
And he has an Indian's craftiness too ;
Now they near him—now they are on
His heels as it were—and now—HE IS GONE !

But where ?
How they stare
And rave and swear !
And how—here, there, and everywhere,
The island they search—for they think, like the deer
Who leaves the forest and takes to the floods,
The smuggler has quitted the lake for the woods !
But all they find is the empty boat,
Which one of the officers pushes afloat :
The fruitless search they at length give o'er,
And Uriah Skinner was never seen more !
'Tis said, that one of the officers swore,
A strong brimstone odor pervaded the shore ?
And another averred that he saw Skinner go
In the clutch of old Nick, to the regions below.

Nearly six years had passed away,
When a Fisherman out in a storm one day,
Was very near making an awful plunge
To become a meal for the pickerel or longe;
But through the mist, gazing eager-eyed,
In the side of an island, a cave he spied,
And in less than a minute, was safe inside.

Very soon passed the storm, and then,
Ere he prepared to go fishing again,
He looked above, beneath, and around,
And what do you think the fisherman found?
Neither a golden nor silver prize,
But a skull with sockets where once were eyes;
Also some bones of arms and thighs,
And a vertebral column of giant size:
How they got there, he couldn't devise,
For he'd only been used to common-place graves,
And knew nought of " organic remains" in caves:
On matters like *those*, his wits were dull,
So he dropped the subject as well as the skull.

                    'Tis needless to say
                    In this later day,
'Twas the smuggler's bones in the cave, that lay:
All I've to add is—the bones in a grave
Were placed, and the cavern was called " SKINNER'S CAVE."

Skinner's Cave.

Between Skinner's Island and the main land, is MINNOW or MINNIE ISLAND, perhaps the latter name refers to its diminutive dimensions. Close to, and arround it is the great fall seining place, thousands of fish being taken from the lake at this place, every year.

Standing on the rocks in front of the Mountain House, an excellent view of ROUND ISLAND is obtained, and certainly, it is one of the most beautiful objects on the lake. On a calm day, the effects of light and shadow are exquisite. In a photograph by Messrs. Gage & Rowell, of St. Johnsbury, (which may be bought at the Mountain House,) these effects are most happily preserved. Nothing can be more perfect than this view, which, whether as it regards foliage, rock, water or island, is first-rate of its class. Round

3

Island is only a mile and a half from the house, and a very pleasant boat ride will give an excellent appetite for the remarkable quantity of berries of various de- scriptions, for which it is remarkable.

Round Island.

CHAPTER IV.

*Ascent of Owl's Head—Maxims for Mountaineers—
Picturesque Rocks—The Old Field—Fern Hollow
—The Toll Gate—Crinoline Chamber—Half-way
Log—Moses' Rock—The Staircases—Refreshment
Hollow—Views from Summit—A Fish Story—Novel
Descent.*

And now, having visited all the islands, suppose we ascend the Owl's Head Mountain, and at one bird's eye glance, observe, as a whole, scenes which we have been describing in detail, as well as countless attractions besides. A few maxims for " Mountaineers," may be in place here.

Ladies—even though it should cost you a parting pang, when preparing for the upward trip, abandon crinoline and hoop—and don't dress yourself as Villikin's Dinah was ordered to—" in gorgeous array." The worse your attire, the better you will feel. Wear stout shoes or boots ; if damp weather, rubbers ; and should you *have* a Bloomer Costume, put it on by all means, for in some parts of the ascent, you will " bless your stars, and think it luxury"—at least you'll find it amazingly convenient.

Provide yourself with a staff some five feet long, a little sharp at the lower end; something in fact, like the Swiss Alpenstock which is shod with iron; this, however, is only necessary where ice has to be crossed, and such is not the case here.

Do not be in a hurry when you set out; take it coolly at first; you will experience the great benefit of thus husbanding your strength when you get half way up, where it will be most needed.

Carry with you some biscuits or sandwiches, and a little tin cup for water—there are several springs on the way up.

These maxims are for ladies; as for the "sterner and stronger" (?) sex, they must get on or up as they best can, without advice from us.

Owl's Head Mountain.

ASCENT OF OWL'S HEAD.

A direction post on the north side of the Mountain
House, indicates the path to the summit. For a little
way the course is tolerably level, but after about ten
minutes walking, the ascent commences in earnest.
On either side the path is bounded by woods, where
the wild bird sings and the squirrel gambols undisturbed. Before long, you perceive before and above
you, a singular rock of very large size, projecting over
the path from the right hand side. This is called
Shelter Rock; a name not altogether inappropriate, as
a large party might find refuge from a shower, beneath
its overhanging portion. We may here mention that
Owl's Head is remarkable for its picturesque rocks.
A very eminent landscape painter remarked to us last
summer, that he had never, anywhere else, met with
such excellent " studies," in this respect, for an artist.
Not far beyond " Shelter," is *High Rock*—a huge mass
of stone crowned with plumy ferns, and half clad with
the greenest moss. A little brook of the purest water
is soon reached—it is this stream which supplies the
fish pond below. The rivulet crossed, after a rather
steep " grade," you hear the .tinkle of cow-bells, and
suddenly enter a large open space, almost circular in
shape and nearly level. After the brisk climbing, the
pathway through the *Old Field*, as it is termed, is a
pleasant change enough. You may, if you choose,
loiter and pick berries—mulberries, blackberries, rasp-
berries &c., and wild flowers, which are very abundant.

Here you have a fine view of one of the mountain ledges, which if you are a sketcher, you will not fail to transfer to your portfolio. Nor will the " Amphitheatre of woods," also visible here, be without its attractions. A "sugar camp" is next passed—in other words, a maple grove ; and then we arrive at a circular sort of basin named *Fern Hollow*—the said basin being quite covered with those plants. Still ascending, we get to *Fern Rock*, where a botanist might long luxuriate. The way now becomes pretty steep, but if you halt occasionally to recover breath, you may use your eyes as well as rest your lungs, for there are plenty of objects worthy attention. For instance, here is *Birch Rock*. On the steep hill-side above you are two large, oblong granite rocks—their ends being placed so close together that there does not appear room to place a finger's point between. Yet in that fissure is sufficient earth to nourish a fine birch tree, which seems to rise from, and grow out of the lower stone. Chester Rock (named after a very intelligent boy guide) is a huge mass of limestone partly covered with moss, and crowned with white pine. Onward and upward we go, until we are brought to a stand at the *Toll-Gate*, where it is by no means an unusual thing to find a toll-keeper also. This Toll-Gate is formed by two large rocks, from whose upper surface trees spring upwards, and between which, there is just room for one very stout, or two very slim persons to walk abreast. Hoops have no chance here, unless the circles are changed into ovals, or elipsis. We have known ladies who were compelled to retire to a leafy bower, hard by, called *Crinoline Chamber*, and divest themselves of their " hindrances," for a Camel may as well attempt to go through the eye of a needle, as a fashionably dressed lady to get through the Toll-Gate. This perilous " pass" having been accomplished, the next object of attraction is the *Chair Rock*, from whose summit the first view of the lake during the ascent, is obtained. Beyond this is *Half-way Log*, where we had better rest; and while we do so, let us state that away to our right, and below us, is one of the most remarkable " bits" of scenery on the mountain ; though as it lies out of the main pathway, but comparatively few stumble on it, except by accident. It may, though, be easily reached from the Mountain House, in half an hour. It is a bold escarpment of rock, forming part of the lower of the two ledges which runs across the mountain's eastern side. Two huge walls of limestone meeting in a V shape, enclose near their bases, a triangular platform, some 12 feet from the ground, on which grow grass and wild flowers. Beneath this verdant shelf is a solid rock, near the centre of the face of which, is a small orifice about the size of a goose-quill, from which a stream of the purest water perpetually flows. How far this natural conduit extends cannot be known. It is a natural curiosity, which would be well worth a visit, even were it not for the grandeur of the rocks which tower high above it.

But by this time we have rested, and are now ready for the " tug" of war. Now are to come the "pinches" as the guides say. Here is the first of them—*Breakneck Stairs*. Do not be alarmed at the name, no one ever dislocated their cervical vertebræ there that we are aware of; nor have we, for already we have surmounted them with sculls as well supported as ever. More stairs! Yes—those we now arrive at are named after an " inferior" portion of the frame. Let us buckle to, and try *Weary-toe Steps*. Not so bad though, as the name seems to imply, but the necessity of using our pedal extremities, *does* make them ache a trifle, thats a fact! Next come *Jennings' Staircase*, and *Winding Staircase*, and then *Refreshment Hollow*, where your little tin can will be found useful in conveying water from the spring to your lips. Somewhat refreshed, we now set out for *Spruce Tree Steps*—the roots of those trees forming the stairs. Then comes *Fountain Ravine*, where you will find a little fountain right in the pathway. The next ascent is named after a curious birch tree on the right. Courage—we are getting near the summit! *Shamrock Rock* and the *Giant's Staircase* are " done," and clear of the forests, we stand on the summit of Owl's Head—nearly 3000 feet above the waters of Memphremagog.

As we rest on one of the crags, a pair of Eagles are seen sailing in the air far below us ; their rich brown plumage and bald white heads gleaming in the sunshine. They build on some of the inaccessible crags

about here. Falcons of many varieties make their
homes on the ledges below. Fish Hawks, a species of
Ospray, too, are common. Last summer, we saw one
of these birds strike a large fish in the lake, opposite
the Mountain House—a fish too large for the winged
angler to carry off after it had killed it. Mr. Jennings
despatched a boat to the scene of slaughter, from
which the Ospray sulkily wheeled away, and a fine
shad of four pounds weight smoked on our breakfast
table next morning. It is not every landlord who has
a bird to provide fish for his guests.

The prospect from Owl's Head summit is magnificent beyond description. On clear days, Montreal can
be distinctly seen. Looking south you see Clyde, Barton and Black Rivers, Newport, all the islands on the
lake, and the lake itself from end to end. To the
north, Durham's Point, Dewey's Point, Knowlton Bay,
the Outlet, Orford Mountain, and countless other objects. To the east, Seymour Lake, Stanstead Plain,
Rock Island, Salem Pond, Charleston Pond, Derby
Centre, Derby line, Willoughby Lake, White Mountains, Little Magog, Massawippee Lake, Georgeville,
&c. To the west, the continuation of the Green
Mountain Range. To the north-west, the Sugar Loaf
and Ridge Mountain, Broome Lake, North and South
Troy, Mansonville, and a mile and a half of wilder-
ness stretching from the base of Owl's Head. These
are but a few of the objects discernable ; we have not
space to mention a tithe of them. But let us exam-

ine the summit itself. As might be expected from its appearance from below, it is all split up, or riven into gorges and ravines, from which four distinct peaks ascend. In one of these ravines is the *Freemason's Lodge*, so named from the fact that the Golden Rule Lodge of Stanstead, hold a lodge there once a year, on the 24th of June. It is a spot well calculated for exercising the mysteries of the craft. On a triangular rock are painted the compass and square, and below that masonic emblem the following inscription :

GOLDEN RULE LODGE,

No. 8, Freemasons of Stanstead, held a Communication here Sept. 10, A. L. '57 and '58.

R. W.　Brother E. Gustin, D. D., G. M., V. W.

B. W.　Rev. H. J. Machin, W. M.

"　　　E. B. Gustin, P. M.

"　　　E. B. Rider,　　"

"　　　A. Bodwell,　　"

"　　　S. Kingsbury, T. I. M.

"　　　C. B. Baxter.

"　　　E. H. Fennessy.

"　　　N. Bachelder.

"　　　A. C. Hall.

"　　　C. S. Channell.

"　　　A. S. Gove.

The descent of the Mountain is comparatively easy. It is remarkable that although so many persons of both sexes have ascended the mountain, no serious accidents have happened; indeed such need not occur, if but common care be taken. A few months since, however, a man named Sabine, had a narrow escape. Near, or rather on the summit is a place called the *Devil's Slide.* ˉDown this, a party of three determined to go, on their way home; two were in port, and these were not a little astounded and dismayed by seeing their companion suddenly shoot by them and suddenly disappear over a ledge, sheer 30 feet deep. He had set out running to overtake his friends and could not stop himself. They of course expected to find him dead and mangled, and cautiously picking their way over the loose stones, at length reached him at the foot of *another* precipice, sixty feet deep, lying face downward, on a bed of broken rocks! Sabine had struck a rocky shelf after his first descent, and bounding off, ball like, went over the second—90 feet in all. His friends finding him motionless, and to all appearance dead, suggested the propriety of getting assistance to take down the body, for " poor fellow, *he's* gone" said one of them. No sooner were the word's uttered, however, than Sabine first lifted one leg, then his head, and said coolly, " Come along boys, this is the quickest way down!" The poor fellow was a good deal hurt, but no bones were broken, and with assistance he descended. A fortnight's care set him to rights again. We said, the

place he shot from was called *Devil's Slide*, but as
there is no record of that sable gentleman's having
performed such an extraordinary feat of " ground and
lofty tumbling," as Mr. Sabine did—the latter is clearly
entitled to have his name substituted for Satan's, and
accordingly Sabine's leap has quite superseded the dia-
bolic appellation.

The mineral riches of Owl's Head have been but im-
perfectly developed. Some years ago, Indians used to
dig there for lead, and in later times, some white people
also commenced workings; but, as in the case of the
Novaculite, the Government stepped in and stopped
proceedings. The Mountain was also the scene of a
hoax, by some scamp who pretended to have had spir-
itual revelations concerning mineral riches there, and
who duped not a few credulous noodles.

CHAPTER V.

Perkins' Landing—Trout Rock—Cedar Point—Mount Elephantis--Ridge Mountain—Concert Pond--Good News for Trout-takers—Knowlton's Landing—Gibraltar Point—Georgeville—The Sea Serpent—Mount Orford—Magog Outlet—Indian Anecdote.

Once more we are aboard the MOUNTAIN MAID, with our faces turned northward; but, before we leave the wharf, let us pay a well deserved compliment to Mr. Jennings, whose Mountain House is really a Model Hotel. Every thing is done to promote the comfort of the guests, and the charges are most moderate. A gentleman who had sojourned there two summers, declared that mosquitoes were things unknown in that locality; he had never seen but one, and that he suspected came passenger on the boat from Newport. His statement we have had ample corroboration of. The only "Varmint" we saw there, was a dead Bear, which had been killed in the woods, back of the Mountain, and very nice eating Master Bruin proved to be. Only fancy, no mosquitoes, no snakes, no hot nights! Who would not summer it in such an Eden?"

Proceeding north, we keep the western shore, and

glide by some magnificent mountain sides, torwards
Perkins' Landing, enjoying a fine echo, as we fire off
our guns and pistols. We pass *Trout Rock*, which
rises from the deepest part of the lake, aslo *Cedar
Point*. After leaving Perkins', which lies in a pretty
bay, turn and view Owl's Head from thence; seen
from the south, its head appeared rounded and jagged;
from this point it is sharp, peaked, and rises cone-like.
It is incomparably the finest and most imposing view
of this Monarch of the lake. Before you, and to the
left, is the next most remarkable Mountain in this
region—*Mount Elephantis*, or as it is sometimes called
Sugar Loaf. The former is doubtless, most correct.

Mt. Elephantis.

Every one will at once discover the resemblance to

an Elephant's head and back, which its upper part presents. Between this and the next, *Ridge Mountain*, is a singular sheet of water, *Concert Pond*, which lies far above the level of the lake. It abounds with delicious Mountain Trout, (pink-fleshed.) How they got there is the question, for there is, we are told, no perceptible inlet to, or outlet from the pond, which is easily reached by an hour's walk from Perkins', or *Knowlton's Landing*, which is the next reached. This is situated at the entrance of *Knowlton's Bay*, an arm of the lake, which stretches inland for a considerable distance. Just after leaving Knowlton's, the Boat passes *Gibraltar Point*, a bold headland, crowned with trees, and picturesque in every respect. Here is the place to see artist passenger out with pencil and sketchbook. Nearly opposite Knowlton's, on the eastern shore, is GEORGEVILLE, which we are now approaching.

It is a pretty, rural village, and a favorite stopping place for artists and anglers. It contains, being a Port of Entry, a Custom House, has a school, one or two stores, some handsome dwellings, chief among which is the Villa of Captain Fogg, and two hotels, one, the Memphremagog House, at which is the Post Office kept by Mr. E. S. Channell, and the other, the Union House, kept by Mr. L. Bigelow—both are extremely comfortable establishments.

On the beach, near Georgeville, very beautiful and perfect crystals of quartz are found; geologists would find here a rich field for their investigations. The fishing opposite the village, for longe, is not to be surpassed, and the woods near, abound with game. The lovers of the marvelous will be perhaps glad to know that the *Sea Serpent* occasionally shows itself somewhere in this locality—that mysterious fish-reptile, being by some, supposed to visit the lake through a hole in its deepest part, and to return by the same subterancan, or sub-aqueous channel, when it desires, for the benefit of its health, to exchange fresh water for salt. We were solemnly assured by one gentleman, that he had actu-ally seen the "critter"—possibly he believed he did—but if Faith can remove Mountains, manufacturing a Sea Serpent must be about as easy as making a Mer-maid, according to the ingenious Mr. Barnum's recipe.

The stage road ride from Georgeville to the outlet is very delightful, and no tourist should fail to hire one of Mr. Channell's teams, and enjoy it.

Mt. Orford.

Leaving Georgeville, we now cross the lake in a "slan-
tindicular" direction—*Mount Orford*, the highest land
in Canada East, rising grandly before us in the distance.
This Mountain is 3,300 feet high, and is surrounded at
its base with a wide belt of forest. It is a favorite
camping ground for sportsmen, all kinds of game being
found there in plenty. The lake, narrowed at Georgeville, now again widens, and *Lord's Island* lies before
us. The next landing is *Paige's*, from whence we again
cross the lake diagonally, and soon arrive at the ter-
mination of our Lake Trip—*Magog Village*, or the *Outlet*, as it is more generally termed.

Here a stage will be found in waiting to convey passengers to *Sherbrooke*, some fifteen miles distant, where
is a depot of the Grand Trunk Railroad, in the cars
of which, Montreal or Quebec may be reached the
same evening. On the road to Sherbrooke, Little Magog Lake is passed, but it possesses no features of peculiar interest.

The village of Magog is but small. It contains a
Catholic Church, a good hotel, kept by Mr. Buck, some
stores, a Post Office, and some extensive saw mills,
the water privilege caused by the fall at the outlet of the
lake, being very fine. Here the Mountain Maid remains
for an hour or two, before her return trip, affording
passengers an opportunity to stroll, or dine.

Magog was once a strong-hold of the Indians, and a
rather interesting story was related to us by one of the
" oldest inhabitants," who had received it traditionally.

4

and doubted not of its truth.   A young and handsome
warrior of the Tribe had committed some offence for
which death was the inevitable punishment.   He ad-
mitted the justice of his sentence ; but only asked one
favor.   It was that he might be permitted to visit an
aged father many miles distant, on his promising to
return on the day fixed for his death.   His request was
granted, and the young " bravo" departed.   Some
months elapsed, and the time of the appointed tortur-
ing process drew near; but all felt sure that the unfor-
tunate youth's word would be kept, and it was ; precisely on the day, at the hour appointed, he marched
into the circle of wigwams, and merely saying " I am
ready;" gave himself up a willing offering to the offended
justice of his Tribe.   Occasionally stone arrow heads
and other Indian relics are dug up at Magog, as they
are also at Owl's Head.

.*. A list (necessarily incomplete,) of some of the principal animals, birds, fishes, and reptiles, to be found in
Lake Memphremagog, and in its vicinity, may not be
uninteresting :—

ANIMALS.

Deer, Bears, Foxes, Squirrels, (various,) Hares, Rab-
bits, Woodchuck, Beaver.

BIRDS.

Eagles, (various,) Falcons, (various,) Hawks, Gulls, Pigeons, Loon, Duck, Partridge, Snipe, Woodcock, Brant, Geese.

FISHES.

Longe, Pickerel, Shadwaiters, Eels, Rock Bass, Cat-Fish, Suckers, Trout.

REPTILES.

Common Green Snake, Black Snake, Chicken Snake, Garter Snake, Toads, Frogs,—(there are no known venomous reptiles—that we are aware of.)

GEOLOGICAL CHARACTERISTICS.

For the Geological Characteristics of the lake shores, we refer the reader to the respective reports of Professor Hitchcock, and Sir William Logan. Details of such would be quite out of place in a *brochure*, such as this.

CLIMATE.

No climate can be more salubrious than that on and about Lake Memphremagog.   Tempests are but seldom experienced, and the air is pure and bracing.   The vicinity of the lake always ensures a sufficiency of moisture in the atmosphere.   The Summers are cool, and the Winters far milder than in Boston or New York.

PRINCIPAL HOTELS IN THE CHIEF CITIES, TOWNS AND VILLAGES ON THE ROUTE TO OR FROM MEMPHREMAGOG.

NEW YORK.—St. Nicholas, Metropolitan, Astor, Everett House, Claredon, &c., &c.

BOSTON.—Revere, Tremont, American House, Parker's, Marlboro'.

SPRINGFIELD.—Massasoit House, American House.

LOWELL.—Merrimack House, American House.

CONCORD.—Phœnix, Eagle, Gass's American House.

WHITE RIVER JUNCTION.—Junction House.

NEWBURY.—Newbury House, Spring Hotel.

ST. JOHNSBURY.—St. Johnsbury House.

BARTON.—Barton Hotel.

NEWPORT.—Memphremagog House.

QUEBEC.—Russell's Hotel.

MONTREAL.—St. Lawrence Hall, Ottawa House, Montreal House.

SHERBROOKE.—Sherbrooke House, Cheney's Hotel.

PORTLAND.—American House, Walnut Street House.

ROUTE TABLE.

From Boston, via. Boston and Maine, Concord, Manchester, and Lawrence, Boston, Concord and Montreal Railroad, and Connecticut and Passumpsic Rivers Railroad to Barton. STATION, HAYMARKET SQUARE, BOSTON.

From Boston, via. Boston and Lowell, Nashua and Lowell, Concord, Northern and Connecticut and Passumpsic Rivers Railroad, up the valleys of the Connecticut and Passumpsic Rivers, to Barton. STATION, CAUSEWAY STREET, BOSTON.

Trains leave Boston by both routes at 7.30 A. M., 12 M., and 5 o'clock, P. M.

Passengers taking 7.30 A. M. train, reach the lake the same evening; those taking 12 M. train, lodge at White River Junction; those taking 5 P. M., train, lodge at Concord, and reach the lake the next evening.

Distance from Boston to Lake Memphremagog.

Railroad, - - - -	232
Stage, - - - - -	14

246 Miles.

Fare $7.50.

From New York, by railroad, via. New Haven, Hartford, Springfield and Bellows Falls. Station, 27th Street.

Trains leave at 8 o'clock, A. M., and 4 o'clock, P. M. Passengers from New York, at 8 o'clock, A. M., can stop over night at Hartford, Springfield, or Northampton, or any other point *above* Hartford, and reach the lake the next evening, at a seasonable hour.

Passengers leaving New York at 4 o'clock, P. M., can stop at the same places over night, and reach the lake as soon as by leaving at 8 o'clock, A. M.

Dine at White River Junction; tea at Barton.

Distance from New York to Lake Memphremagog.
Railroad, - - - - 352
Stage, - - - - - 14
—————
366 Miles.

Fare, $10.25.

WHITE AND FRANCONIA MOUNTAINS

TO

LAKE MEMPHREMAGOG.

Leave the White Mountains at 6 o'clock, A. M.
" " Franconia " " 7 o'clock, A. M.

By Stage, to Littleton, thence by White Mountains
Railroad to Wells River, dine at the Coossuck House, or
Newbury, at which latter village are the "Sulphur
Springs," and two good Hotels; arriving at 10.30 A.
M., tourists can dine, take the up train of the Connecticut and Passumpsic Rivers Railroad, at 3. 45 P. M.,
sup at Barton, thence by stage to the lake the same
evening. Tickets and *reliable information* can be
had of the Agent of the Connecticut and Passumpsic
Rivers Railroad at the White Mountains, and the Franconia Mountains.

Fare from White Mountains, $5.55.

Distance 115 miles.

Fare from Franconia Mountains, $4.80.

Distance 102 miles.

Tickets can also be bought at a *reduced rate*, by Excursionists, for the round trip, from either of the Mountains, to *Quebec, or Montreal, and back*, to Wells River, or White River Junction.

FROM LAKE MEMPHREMAGOG

TO

QUEBEC AND MONTREAL.

Leave Newport at 7 o'clock, A. M., by Steamer Mountain Maid, Capt. Fogg, to the Outlet, (30 miles,) thence by stage, to Sherbrooke, (15 miles,) dine, take cars of the Grand Trunk Railway, and reach either of above cities same evening.

Returning, leave Quebec at 5.45 A. M., Montreal at 7 o'clock, A. M., by Grand Trunk Railway; dine at Sherbrooke, thence by stage to the Outlet, take Steamer, touching at the " *Mountain House*," lodge at Newport, and thence next morning, by stage to Barton; Connecticut and Passumpsic Rivers Railroad to the Mountains, Boston or New York, same evening, five hours quicker than by any other route.